DATE DUE

DUMP TRUCKS

by Amanda Doering Tourville
illustrated by Zachary Trover

Content Consultant:
Paul M. Goodrum, PE, PhD, Associate Professor
Department of Civil Engineering, University of Kentucky

magic
wagon

visit us at www.abdopublishing.com

Published by Magic Wagon, a division of the ABDO Group, 8000 West 78th Street, Edina, Minnesota, 55439. Copyright © 2009 by Abdo Consulting Group, Inc. International copyrights reserved in all countries. All rights reserved. No part of this book may be reproduced in any form without written permission from the publisher.

Looking Glass Library™ is a trademark and logo of Magic Wagon.

Printed in the United States.

Text by Amanda Doering Tourville
Illustrations by Zachary Trover
Edited by Patricia Stockland
Cover and interior design by Emily Love

Library of Congress Cataloging-in-Publication Data
Tourville, Amanda Doering, 1980-
  Dump trucks / by Amanda Doering Tourville ; illustrated by Zachary Trover.
     p. cm. — (Mighty machines)
  Includes bibliographical references and index.
  ISBN 978-1-60270-623-1
  1. Dump trucks—Juvenile literature. I. Trover, Zachary, ill. II. Title.
  TL230.15.T764 2009
  629.225—dc22
                             2008035998

Table of Contents

What Are Dump Trucks?

Dump trucks are machines that move and dump large loads. Dump trucks move sand, gravel, and rock. Once a dump truck gets into place, its large bed is pushed up. This allows the load to slide out.

Types of Dump Trucks

Most dump trucks unload from the back end of the truck. These trucks are called end dump trucks.

Side dump trucks dump their loads to the side. The driver tilts the bed so that it tips on its side.

Bottom dump trucks empty their loads from the belly of the truck. The load slides through a hole in the truck's underside.

End Dump Truck

Side Dump Truck

Bottom Dump Truck

Off-highway dump trucks are huge. These trucks are too big to drive on roads and highways. Off-highway dump trucks are shipped in pieces to where they are needed. The pieces are put together on-site. These giant dump trucks are used in mines and in quarries.

Highway dump trucks are smaller. They can move from place to place on roads and highways. Highway dump trucks mostly work at construction sites. They haul sand, gravel, and rock.

Parts of Dump Trucks

The bed of a dump truck holds the load. Other machines fill the dump truck's bed with dirt, rock, sand, snow, or other materials. When the load is ready to be dumped, one or two arms push up the bed. Then, the load slides out.

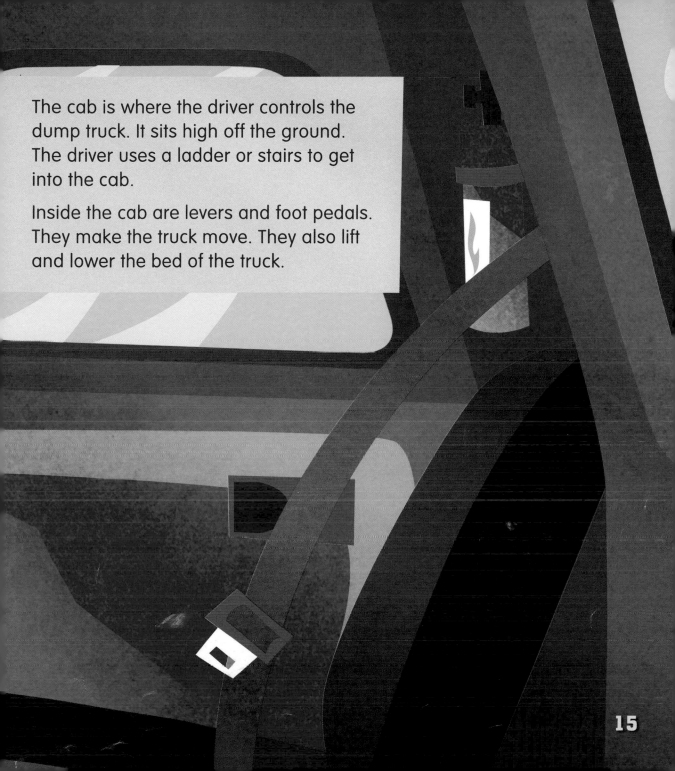

The cab is where the driver controls the dump truck. It sits high off the ground. The driver uses a ladder or stairs to get into the cab.

Inside the cab are levers and foot pedals. They make the truck move. They also lift and lower the bed of the truck.

Most dump trucks have a canopy connected to the bed. This metal cover shields the dump truck's cab. Dump trucks sometimes work in dangerous places. The canopy protects the driver from falling objects.

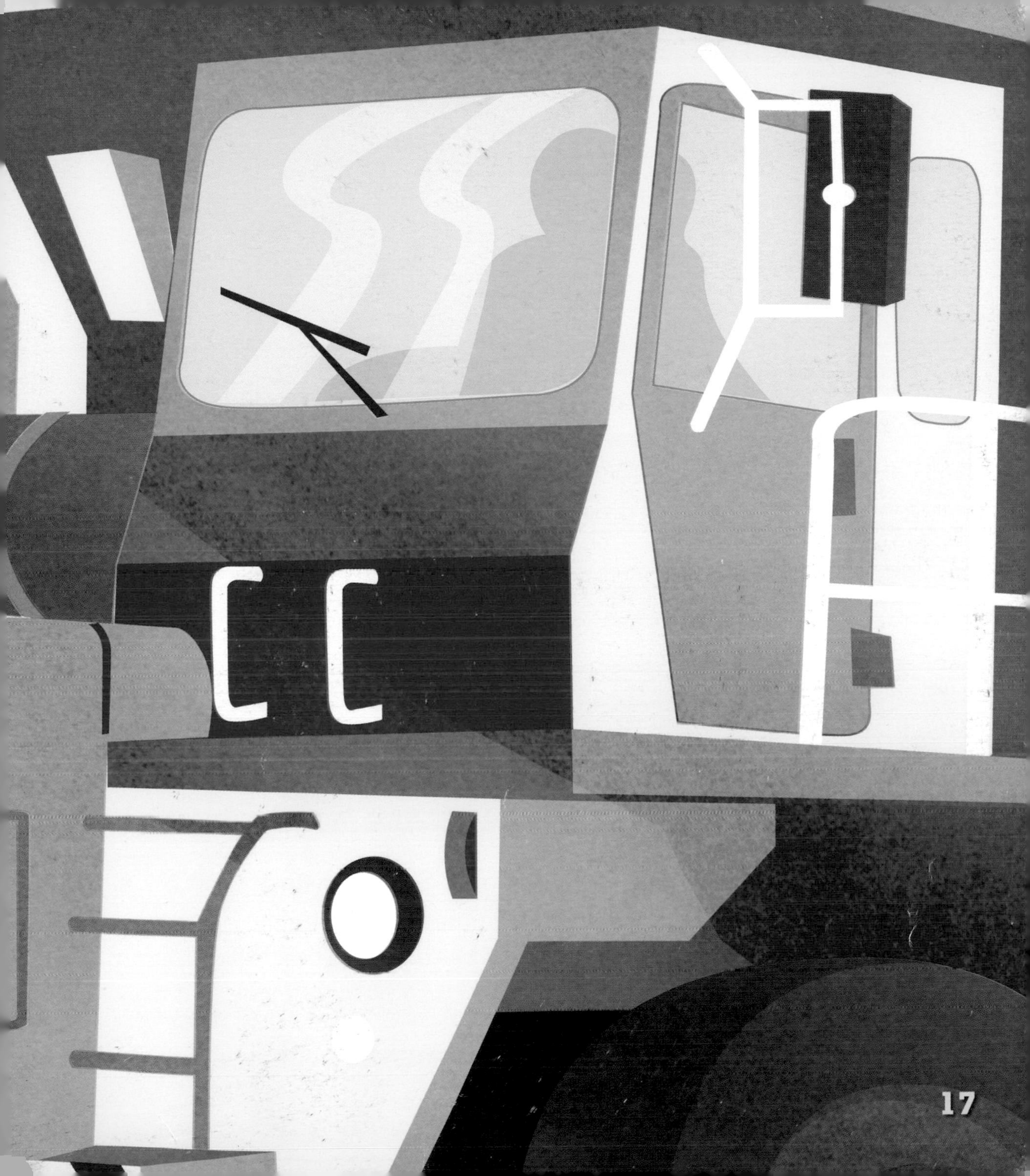

Dump trucks move on very large tires. The tires can be taller than two adults! Many times, dump trucks have two sets of back tires. These tires keep the trucks from slipping. Extra tires also help the trucks carry heavier loads.

How Are Dump Trucks Used?

Most dump trucks are used at construction sites or in mines. At construction sites, dump trucks haul dirt, sand, gravel, and rock. Dump trucks help make buildings and roads. At mines and quarries, dump trucks haul stone, coal, and metal.

Dump trucks also clean up after natural disasters. After a hurricane, earthquake, or tornado, dump trucks haul away tree branches and ruined buildings. After a blizzard, dump trucks haul away snow. Dump trucks help towns and cities get back to normal after a storm.

Where Are Dump Trucks Used?

Dump trucks are used all over the world. They work in underground mines. They haul coal and stone. And, they work in big cities to build roads and haul away snow.

Dump Trucks Are Mighty Machines!

Dump trucks help with construction. They haul materials out from the earth. They help clean up after natural disasters. Dump trucks use strength to haul tons of material to wherever it is needed. Dump trucks are mighty machines!

27

Dump Truck Parts

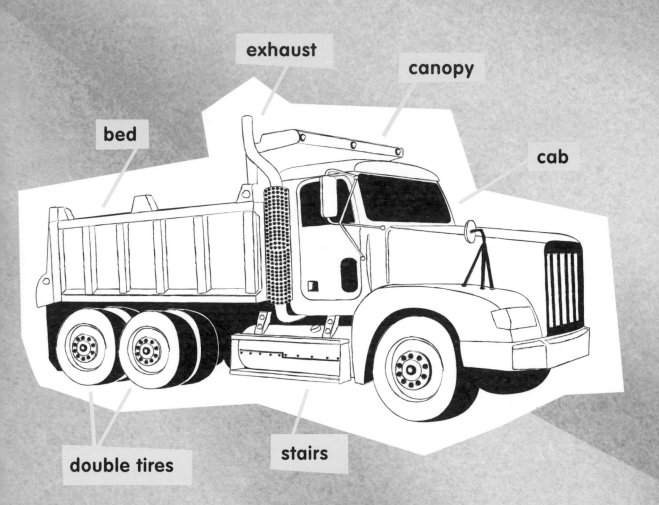

exhaust

canopy

bed

cab

double tires

stairs

End Dump Truck

28

canopy

cab

bed

ladder

double tires

End Dump Truck

29

Fun Facts

- Some dump trucks bend in the middle. These are called articulated dump trucks. They are built in two pieces so that they can turn easily.

- Some dump trucks hold more than 1,000 gallons (3,785 L) of fuel. That's about 50 times the amount of a large car!

- The first dump trucks were created in the 1910s. Workers used a hand crank to lift the beds of these old trucks.

- In some dump trucks, the drivers sit more than 20 feet (6 m) off the ground.

- Dump trucks aren't as fast as cars. Most dump trucks can only travel about 30 to 40 miles per hour (48 to 64 km/h).

- Dump trucks are used to haul gold and diamonds from mines.

Glossary

construction—the act of building or making something.

dangerous—able or likely to harm a person.

disaster—a sudden event that causes destruction and suffering or loss of life. Natural disasters include events such as hurricanes, tornadoes, and earthquakes.

gravel—small pieces of rock.

quarry—an open area that contains stone used for building.

tilt—to move into a slanted position.

Web Sites

To learn more about dump trucks, visit ABDO Group online at **www.abdopublishing.com**. Web sites about dump trucks are featured on our Book Links page. These links are routinely monitored and updated to provide the most current information available.

Index